No Catnapping in the Kitchen

No Catnapping in the Kitchen

Kitty Cat Cuisine

Written by
Wendy Nan Rees

Illustrations by
Hillary Huber Wilson

HOWELL BOOK HOUSE
NEW YORK

Howell Book House
A Simon & Schuster Macmillan Company
1633 Broadway
New York, NY 10019-6785

Macmillan is a registered trademark of Macmillan, Inc.

Library of Congress Cataloging-in-Publication Data
Rees, Wendy Nan.
No catnapping in the kitchen : kitty cat cuisine / written by Wendy Nan Rees :
illustrations by Hillary Huber Wilson.
p.   cm.
Includes index.
ISBN 0-87605-695-8 (alk. paper)
1. Cats—Food—Recipes.   2. Cats—Anecdotes.   I. Title
SF447.6.R44   1996
636/8'08'5—dc20   96-13962
                  CIP

BOOK DESIGN BY GEORGE J. McKEON

I dedicate this book to my good friend and sister-in-law, Liz Rees—a true cat lover. May she have many hours of enjoyment cooking for her two kings, Ernesto and the "Little One."

—WENDY NAN REES

To my best friend and husband, Hoadley. Thanks for enduring the queen of all trades! Have we come full circle? I love you. . . .

—H.H.W.

CONTENTS

Contents

ABOUT THE AUTHOR

Since she was two years old, Wendy Nan Rees has loved animals. Her first pets were an English Setter named Digby and a pony named Ricky, and over the years she's grown attached to many more dogs, cats, horses—you name it. Now her love of animals and her concern for their health and well-being have led Wendy to become an entrepreneur and author. She is the creator of Lip Smackers, a company dedicated to providing healthy, all-natural treats for pets. She has also written a book on how and why people name their pets called *The Name Game*. Wendy lives in Los Angeles with her husband Tom and her two best friends, Governor and Stella Bella.

About the Illustrator

Hillary Huber Wilson is a freelance artist who lives in Los Angeles with her family and her dog, Racine. Having spent the better part of her artistic career in painting, ceramics and graphic design, she is now turning her attention to illustration.

ACKNOWLEDGMENTS

Special thanks to my best friend and husband, Tom Rees. This book could not have happened without his everlasting love, support and great ideas! We had many fun hours charting the adventures of Lola and Tara. Thank you. I love you.

Special thanks to my editor, Ariel Cannon. Your support and patience are everlasting!

To my sister, Carol Ann Blinken Emquies—thank you for being there at every turn. I love you!

Hillary Huber Wilson, you are so talented. A million thanks!

Many thanks to Steve LuKanic, Dot Stovall, Suzie Fairchild and Cathy Stanley.

Lewis and Paula Turner, you have been such an inspiration, providing me with great tips and information, but most of all your friendship.

To my family and friends, thank you for believing in my dreams and always supporting me. Without you I'd be lost.

INTRODUCTION

Even while I was writing my first book, *No Barking at the Table* (a cookbook for dogs), I knew in the back of my mind I wanted to write a special cookbook for cats as well. "You are what you eat" definitely applies to our four-legged feline friends as well.

Obviously, cats' diet requirements are different from dogs'. They need more fats, protein, B vitamins, beta carotene and specific amino acids in order to grow strong and stay healthy.

Cats are carnivores. In the wild, they could literally live their entire lives without ever eating a fruit or vegetable. The animals they would kill and eat provided enough of these types of nutrients as a result of their own omnivorous diets. And, while domesticated cats do enjoy a mixed variety of food, it is the amino acids, vitamins and fat found in meat and fish that are absolutely essential to the cat's existence.

Cats also require higher levels of protein from meat because it provides them with the amino acid taurine. Without taurine, cats would go blind, so it is obviously a very important element in their diet. Taurine also helps prevent—believe it or not—heart disease in cats! So, unlike humans, it is good for cats to eat a lot of meat.

It is no accident that cats absolutely love fish and you may have noticed that many canned cat foods are fish and liver flavored. This is important because both fish and liver have a high vitamin A content. Cats cannot manufacture vitamin A from fruits, vegetables and grains as other animals can, so these meats provide a very important nutrient for cats.

Cats like their food at room temperature. In the wild, cats would make a kill and eat it instantly. Many pet owners store half-opened cans of food in the refrigerator and can't understand why their furry loved ones don't dig right in when they're served. While it *is* necessary to store leftovers in the fridge, your pet may act somewhat hesitant or disinterested until the food warms up a bit. So if the food is overheated or too cold, don't take it too personally—just wait for it to get to room temperature.

And, because cats are hunters by nature, they prefer their food fresh. Cats' sense of smell is actually *four times* more acute than ours, so they can recognize if their food is even slightly "off" or stale. This is a strong instinct in cats and explains their "finicky" eating habits. So if you have a finicky eater, check the food for freshness and temperature.

Perhaps the most valuable reason for reading this book is that most cats' taste preferences are learned by the age of six months. It is important to start your cat out early with a variety of foods so that he or she develops a taste for a well-balanced diet. If cats are served only one type of food or flavor for a long period of time, they may actually lose their ability to enjoy other foods and consequently the nutritional benefits of those foods. If you don't vary your cat's diet from the time he's a kitten, he may get so used to the one flavor or food he is served regularly that he won't be *able* to have an appetite for other foods. This could have a negative effect on his long-term health picture—so develop a varied menu of foods for him at a young age!

About the Recipes

The nutritional requirements for cats are very complex. These recipes are intended to enhance your cat's diet with a fun and healthy variety of foods. A good brand-name dry food will provide your cat with most of the important vitamins and minerals he needs. As an alternative or supplement to canned food, however, *No Catnapping in the Kitchen* offers you a terrific variety of quick and simple recipes that will keep your kitty purring for more!

All these recipes can be frozen in single-serving portions. I have found it is better to defrost your cat's food in the refrigerator before warming it in the oven or the stove in order to prevent overcooking. The microwave can also overheat or overcook your cat's food, so take care if you are using one. And remember to always serve your cat's food from warm to room temperature—never hot.

A Few Dietetic No-Nos

The one thing I have found that dogs and cats *do* have in common regarding diet requirements is that they should never have chocolate—in any amount. Chocolate contains theobromine which can be toxic and, in extreme circumstances (and large doses), fatal.

Cats and onions don't mix well either. An enzyme found in onions can be detrimental to a cat's metabolism, so avoid onions at all cost.

Milk is an obvious mainstay for kittens, but what most people *don't* know is that after approximately three months of age a cat's milk intake should be restricted to very small amounts. At about this age, kittens stop producing enough lactase (the enzyme used to break down the lactose in dairy products) and drinking milk can cause diarrhea.

Lastly, be sure to avoid raw meat, raw fish and raw eggs. These carry bacteria that can cause illness in pets and humans.

With new treats, food products, or diet changes, always consult your veterinarian to make sure they are correct and healthy choices for your pet.

BEFORE YOU BEGIN

Listed below are a few tips and helpful hints that will help make life easy in the kitchen when it comes to preparing food for your pet.

Many of the recipes in this book call for boiled chicken livers or boiled chicken pieces. In a large sauce pan or stock pot add approximately 5 cups of cold water per each pound of meat. Add a bay leaf for flavor. Bring contents to a boil and simmer for 25 to 30 minutes uncovered. Drain and remove bay leaf. Serve plain or as suggested in other recipes.

So that you can prepare many recipes quickly, I strongly suggest cooking a few pounds of chicken or liver per the above means and then freezing a number of single-size portions. Use freezer bags or freezer containers and then simply use them as needed with the recipes.

Other recipes call for fish stock. Fish stock is very easy to make at home and can also be frozen in single-serving portions. For fish stock: 2 pounds fish trimmings (bones, heads, tails and some meat), 1 carrot, chopped, 1 celery stalk (with leaves), chopped, 1 bunch parsley, 6 cups water. Rinse the fish trimmings well, place in large stock pot, bring to a boil then simmer for 35 to 40 minutes. Strain liquid, cool and serve or freeze for recipe use. In a real pinch for fish stock, use bottled clam juice.

Here's a lifesaver that will keep you from having to run to the market. When fresh fish is hard to come by, use freeze-dried fish. Place dried fish in a bowl, add boiling water, let sit for 20 to 30 minutes and drain. Freeze-dried fish will stay good in your cabinet for years.

Freeze-dried fish powder is also included in many of the recipes. You can find it in the specialty department of your local supermarket.

Believe it or not, cats also like parsley. Chopped parsley not only tastes great but contains chlorophyll which helps freshen breath (halitosis can be a real problem for some cats). Parsley can be added to any recipe. This is a must if you've got an affectionate "facelicker"!

You can purchase brewer's yeast at a health-food store. Feel free to add this to any recipe (like the cookie recipes) since many people claim it helps control fleas and aids in digestion.

Many of my recipes call for beef or chicken broth. I prefer the low-salt versions purchased from the supermarket.

GROW YOUR OWN CATNIP

Most cats absolutely love catnip, a derivative of the mint plant. It is available in many forms: dried in toys or fresh off the plant for consumption. Catnip is a healthy and fun treat for your cat, but should always be used in measured doses.

Interestingly, almost one-third of all cats do not respond to catnip at all. Those that do respond may also react just as strongly to the fragrance of shampoos and lotions. Generally, most cats will *not* have a reaction to catnip until after the age of six months.

You can add catnip to any of the treat recipes, and this entertaining herb is fun and economical to grow at home. Catnip seeds are available at pet stores and at your local nursery. Sprinkle a few in a terra-cotta pot with soil, water and watch them grow.

THE "TAIL" OF LOLA AND TARA (AND THEIR FAVORITE RECIPES)

This is the story about two cats, Lola and Tara, and an incident that led to the adventure of their lives. Here is their story, as Lola remembers it some years later (with some help from their daily journal, in which they jotted down more than a few recipes).

. . . .

It was a Sunday afternoon in late June. Our owners ("Mom" and "Dad" to us) had been anxiously awaiting the arrival of great Aunt Millie and Uncle George, who were returning from a vacation cruise they had planned for a lifetime. The trip aboard a luxury oceanliner had originated in London, England, and was ending here in our hometown of Long Beach, California.

We all loaded into our car that Sunday and headed off to the Long Beach "Port of Entry"—the main harbor—where huge ships come and go daily from all parts of the world.

Now I just love going for an outdoor adventure in the car; in fact, I get excited doing just about *anything* that gets me out of the house. That's where my long-time companion and best friend, Tara, and I really differ.

I'm outgoing, vivacious and love "the good life." Diamonds are my best friend (I have a diamond-studded collar) and caviar is my all-time favorite. I mean, you only have nine lives, so you might as well live them to the fullest, right?

Tara hates to go out of the house, and the car makes her especially sick. The outdoors scare her to death and the mere thought of leaving her warm window seat really disrupts her life. Can you imagine? She loves TV and the mundane home life. We couldn't be more different, but at the same time we have been together for ten years and other than a rare "cat fight," we get along fabulously.

Originally, Mom and Dad only wanted one cat, but they couldn't pick between Tara and me, so they brought both of us home! I'm Siamese, with long legs, blue eyes and a coat like a mink. From the very start I was the verbal one, always talking and getting into trouble. Tara is an orange tabby with big green eyes and a belly the size of a bear. She is little "Miss Goodie Two-Shoes." Her only vice is a tendency to overeat. She's never picky about her food, and she literally eats everything in sight—even *my* leftovers.

On this fateful June afternoon, Mom, Dad and I lured Tara into the car with a snack and off we went. When we arrived at the docks, Tara and I were told to wait in the car, but I could hardly keep my eyes in my head. I had always wanted to see a ship, but this ship was grander

than any I had ever imagined! Despite my whining invitations to inspect the ship a little more closely, Tara just wanted to sleep in the car until they got back. She wouldn't budge until I enticed her with "Look at all the crates of *food* going onto that boat! It smells like shrimp and lobster!" That's all it took. In a flash, we slipped out through one of the partially opened windows.

This seemingly innocent move changed our lives forever. What you're about to read is our account of this amazing adventure and the delicious foods we encountered on our travels. We hope you and your cats will enjoy our stories and favorite recipes from around the world as much as we did, and still do!

1

The South Pacific

The Awful Beginning

The boat is huge! We're hiding down below deck. Tara is seasick and she can't even move today. My heart is pounding too, but I love the thrill. I know we'll be okay. We have water, but I have to find some food. All Tara can say is "How did this happen? How is it we didn't get off this boat in time?" I have to take care of Tara now. Will write more tomorrow . . .

Tara isn't any better today. Water is all she wants, and it's a good thing because that's all we have. I went on the hunt late last night. No food, but I found out we're on the *Queen Mary* headed around the world for ninety days! When I told Tara she just about died—"I want to go home, Lola!" Complain, complain, complain. Our first stop will be an island called Hawaii. Alo-HA! I can't wait! . . .

Tara finally found her sea legs, so we went for a walk today. The fresh air has done us both a world of good. Water is still not a problem, but food is hard to come by. We need to keep a low profile so we don't get caught, but we must make friends with someone in the kitchen. I'm so hungry, even Tara's starting to look tasty. We arrive in Hawaii tomorrow. Let there be food!

Hawaii

THE PORT OF HONOLULU, HAWAII

What a glorious day! The water is blue, the sky is too, and the sun couldn't be brighter. We're so excited to get off this boat—Tara has been doing *nothing* but complaining. Can't wait to EAT!!

We finally stole away from the ship for awhile. Boy, were people friendly! Outdoor restaurants galore! Tara was so stuffed after three hours of eating she could hardly climb the plank back up to the ship!

We learned today that the English navigator, Captain James Cook, first discovered these islands in 1778. He named them "The Sandwich Islands," which is what they were called until they were renamed in the nineteenth century.

We didn't eat any sandwiches, but here was one of our favorite dishes ashore:

Fish Moli

6-8 servings

1 clove garlic, crushed

1 teaspoon butter

a little ginger

1/2 ounce flour

1/4 cup coconut milk

salt to taste

1 pound fish

1/4 teaspoon turmeric

Fry the garlic in the butter with the ginger. Stir in the flour and cook slowly for 3 minutes. Add the coconut milk and salt. Stir slowly until the mixture comes to a boil. Add the fish and the turmeric. Let simmer for 20 to 30 minutes, or until the fish is well cooked. Serve warm.

Tonga

We loved Hawaii and now we're going to an island called Tonga. We've made friends with a young cook in the ship's kitchen and once a day he brings us leftovers to hold us from port to port.

Boy, do the people here like to eat! We heard the Tongan king weighs over five hundred pounds, and that the heavier you are, the higher your social stature! Tara could be a queen here!

Tongan Fish Salad

4-6 servings

1 fish (about 2 pounds), boiled and cooled

pepper

4 cloves garlic

2 tablespoons olive oil

1 teaspoon vinegar

coconut cream

1 lettuce leaf

2 eggs, hard-boiled

Wash fish well, bone and skin it. Cut into small cubes. Poach for 20 to 30 minutes until done. Place it in a pie dish, sprinkle with a little pepper and mix well. Mince the garlic and the fish. Add the oil and vinegar. Cover with coconut cream and serve with lettuce and egg.

NOTE: We always enjoy our Polynesian dishes with a small glass of Okolehao, which is made from molasses, rice and taro, fermented and distilled. Like red wine with French food, I'm sure it's very good for us.

Gammon Steak Tahitian

6-8 servings

1/3 cup soft light brown sugar

1/4 cup butter or margarine

4 tablespoons red wine vinegar

1 1/2 pounds smoked
gammon steak,
cut 1/2-3/4 inch thick

4 firm bananas

optional garnish: watercress

Heat the sugar, butter or margarine and vinegar in a large frying pan until the sugar has dissolved and the butter melted. Stir frequently.

Add the gammon steak to the pan. Cook for 5 minutes on each side or until cooked through.

Remove the steak while you prepare the bananas.

Peel the bananas and cut them into 1 1/2-inch pieces. Add to the sugar-and-vinegar syrup in the frying pan.

Cook the bananas for about 5 minutes or until heated through, spooning the syrup over them all the time.

Spoon the bananas around the gammon steak and pour remaining sauce over the steak and fruit. Serve garnished with watercress if you wish.

Fiji

Tara was terrified of Fiji before getting off the boat. She knew that in 1643, when the island was originally discovered by a Dutch explorer named Abel Tasman, the native people had a reputation for being savage cannibals. To her surprise, the people were warm and friendly, the food was delightful and we will never forget the "Blue Lagoon" (where they actually filmed the movie!).

Polynesian Seaweed Salad

4-6 servings

1/2 ounce seaweed

1 cup cucumber

1 small head lettuce

2 tablespoons wine or cider vinegar

3 tablespoons sesame oil

3 tablespoons low-salt soy sauce

Soak seaweed in boiling water for 5 minutes. Drain. Cover with cold water and leave for 10 minutes. Then drain thoroughly. Thinly slice the cucumber and shred the lettuce. Put all the salad ingredients into a bowl. Stir together the vinegar, sesame oil and soy sauce. Spoon over the salad and serve at once.

Shton

(WHITE BAIT OMELET)

2–3 servings

4–5 ounces white bait

4 eggs, beaten

1 handful chopped parsley

1/2 teaspoon salt

1/2 teaspoon pepper

8 tablespoons olive oil

Prepare the white bait. Mix together the eggs, parsley, salt and pepper. Cook the fish in the oil with 2 tablespoons water. Then pour in the egg mixture and stir gently until the egg is set.

Australia

G'day mates and no worries! Australians sure talk funny, but what a fun people they are. The British used to send all their prison convicts here, so maybe that's why the "Aussies" seem to enjoy the outdoors so much!

South Seas Fish in Foil

Foil is used as a substitute for the large leaves of various tropical plants. These leaves or husks of sweet corn could also be used.

6–8 servings

6 trout or any white fish (1/2–3/4 pounds)

6 tablespoons melted butter

2 teaspoons soy sauce

juice of 1 lemon

1/2 teaspoon ground ginger

1/2 pound fresh spinach leaves, washed

Preheat oven to 350 degrees.

Clean and wash fish. Stir together melted butter, soy sauce and lemon juice. Brush on fish, inside and out. Sprinkle lightly with ginger.

Place a few spinach leaves on a square of aluminum foil. Lay a seasoned serving of fish on spinach and place a few leaves on top. Wrap in foil, turning the ends in and folding securely.

Place on a shallow baking tray and bake for 30 to 40 minutes.

Kangaroo Hoppers

20-30 small balls

1/2 pound shrimp, cleaned

1 tablespoon kelp powder

1 tablespoon wheat germ

1/2 teaspoon vegetable oil

1 clove garlic, chopped

1 cup crushed corn flakes

Preheat oven to 350 degrees.

Clean and de-vein shrimp. Boil until pink and cooked through. When cool, puree shrimp, add kelp powder, wheat germ, vegetable oil and garlic. Roll into balls then roll in the corn flakes to coat shrimp mixture. Bake on lightly greased cookie sheet for 10 to 15 minutes. Cool and serve.

Store in airtight container in refrigerator.

2

Asia

Soy sauce, soy sauce and more soy sauce! We had never tried it before, but now it seems to be in every single thing we eat, and we absolutely love it. Chopsticks, however, are more of a problem . . . .

Japan

Sushi is a big deal over here but since raw fish doesn't agree with us, we lived on these great fish cake cookies. Wow!

Fish Cake Cookies

**20–30 cookies depending on size.
We prefer them small and ladylike.**

1 can dark tuna, packed in oil

1 teaspoon kelp powder

1 teaspoon shrimp powder

1 cup bread crumbs

1 teaspoon soy sauce

1 egg, beaten

Preheat oven to 325 degrees.

Blend tuna, kelp powder, shrimp powder and bread crumbs. Add egg and mix well. Drop by 1/2 teaspoon onto greased cookie sheet and bake 7 to 10 minutes until done. Cool and serve. May be frozen for later use or stored in an airtight container in the refrigerator.

Hong Kong

The port of Hong Kong is the busiest in all the world (and we thought Long Beach was hoppin'). Tara and I almost missed the boat because we couldn't stop shopping. I've never seen so many clothing and electronics stores all in one place—and talk about bargains! Best of all, everything is "duty free"!

We did, of course, manage to find some good restaurants and fun recipes . . . .

Beef with Broccoli

4 servings

1 teaspoon chopped garlic

4 tablespoons peanut oil

1 cup chopped broccoli

1 teaspoon chopped ginger

1 teaspoon soy sauce

1 cup sliced flank steak*

Sauce:

1 teaspoon arrow root

2 tablespoons soy sauce

1 teaspoon brown sugar

1 teaspoon sesame oil

3 tablespoons beef stock

In a wok or frying pan stir-fry garlic in 1 tablespoon peanut oil. Add broccoli. Stir-fry for 3 to 4 minutes. Remove to a separate dish. Add 1 tablespoon peanut oil to wok. Stir-fry ginger with soy sauce. Add beef and the remaining peanut oil and stir-fry for 5 minutes. Add broccoli and garlic to pan. Combine all sauce ingredients in a bowl and add to pan. Stir-fry until sauce thickens slightly.

Serve over kitty kibble at room temperature.

*To aid in slicing flank steak, freeze it for 45 minutes.

Fried Rice

6 servings

3 tablespoons vegetable oil

1/2 cup cooked chunked carrots

1/2 cup cooked peas

1/2 cup chunked ham

2 cups cold cooked brown rice

1 tablespoon low-salt soy sauce

In a large skillet, heat oil. Add carrots. Sauté until carrots are cooked. Add peas, ham, rice and soy sauce. Cook for 10 minutes over medium heat while stirring. Serve cool.

China

We've never seen so many people in one place in all our lives. Tara's tail got run over by someone on a bicycle. I'm not surprised, though—she's gained so much weight she couldn't move out of the way fast enough. We've tried to eat a little lighter on this trip ashore. Here are some of our favorites.

Chinese Chicken Salad

6–8 servings

3 cups shredded cooked chicken

1 small red bell pepper, cut into julienne strips

Dressing:

1 tablespoon soy sauce

1 tablespoon hoisin sauce

2 tablespoons water

2 tablespoons chicken broth

1 teaspoon corn oil

Blend all ingredients.

A Brown Rice Fit to Be Fed

We love white rice, but discovered a new variety . . . brown rice!

4 servings

2 cups low-salt beef broth

1 cup instant brown rice

1 tablespoon chopped garlic

In a medium sauce pan, bring beef broth to a boil. Add remaining ingredients. Cover and simmer for 20 minutes. Recipe may be doubled.

China Chips

6-8 servings

1/2 pound cooked boneless chicken, white and dark meat

1/2 cup dried shrimp powder

2 cloves garlic

1 cup low-salt chicken broth

1 1/2 cups wheat germ

2 tablespoons brewer's yeast (optional)

2 cups whole-wheat flour (more may be needed)

1 cup yellow cornmeal

garlic powder

Glaze:

Beat 1 egg. Lightly brush on cookie before baking.

Preheat oven to 350 degrees.

In a large blender or food processor, gradually purée chicken, shrimp powder and garlic, slowly adding chicken broth. Transfer the chicken purée into a large bowl. Mix in wheat germ and brewer's yeast. Slowly add flour and cornmeal until the dough becomes stiff. Knead the dough for 3 to 5 minutes. Let it rest for 5 to 10 minutes. On a lightly floured surface, roll the dough into a ball.

As cats like their crackers thin, I have found that the best way to do this is to split the ball into four sections and roll each section into a hot dog shape. Wrap these in plastic wrap and chill for 30 minutes. Slice into very thin chips. Place the chips on a lightly greased cookie sheet (cooking spray is useful for this). Lightly brush each chip with glaze and sprinkle with garlic powder. Bake for 25 to 40 minutes. Halfway through, turn. As the crackers cool, they will become hard. Leftover dough can be frozen for up to 3 months.

Thailand

Thailand is a lush and green country, with beautiful people, wonderful scenery and, of course, food. The word "Thai" actually means "free," which is exactly how we feel about treating ourselves to the seafood here.

Thai Seafood Dinner

4 servings

1 can chopped clams, undrained

1 can anchovies, undrained

1 teaspoon chopped garlic

1/2 teaspoon chopped ginger

1 tablespoon Thai fish sauce (found in the Asian food section at your market)

1 tablespoon brewer's yeast

3 tablespoons cooked brown rice

Blend everything together in a sauce pan. Warm through, then serve.

3

The Indian Ocean

India

Another day, another port! The excitement—and the food—never end. Today we are docking at Madras, an Indian city on the east coast. The Indian temples are supposed to be absolutely beautiful, and there are lots of elephants roaming around (they're considered sacred) so we have to take great care not to get stepped on!

Bombay Pudding

8 servings

2 1/2 pints milk

2 1/2 tablespoons semolina

2 ounces fresh butter

Boil milk. Add semolina and stir until it becomes thick. Stir in the butter and pour into a pie pan. Allow to cool and set.

Dust over with flour and fry in lard, butter or drippings. Cut into three-cornered pieces as you would a tea cake and serve.

Kebabs

(SKEWERED CROQUETTES)

Makes 15–20 kebabs

1 pound ground beef

2 tablespoons mixed herbs

2 tablespoons lemon juice

1 1/2 teaspoons salt

1/2 teaspoon ground ginger

a little oil

Mix all the ingredients except the oil. Form the mixture into small sausage shapes and put these on skewers. Brush the kebabs with oil and grill them, turning frequently until brown.

These may be frozen before or after cooking.

Tandoori Chicken

4 servings

2 boneless chicken breasts

Marinade:

1/2 teaspoon chopped fresh ginger

3 cloves garlic, chopped

1/2 cup plain yogurt

1/2 teaspoon turmeric

1/2 teaspoon paprika

1/3 cup olive oil

Combine all the marinade ingredients in a blender and blend until smooth. Pour over chicken and marinate for 4 to 6 hours.

Grill chicken for 15 minutes on each side until done. Cut into strips and serve over kitty kibble at room temperature.

The Islands of the Maldives

Well, now we've died and gone to heaven, and died and gone to heaven again! The Maldives are a paradise of palm trees, white-sand beaches and bluish-green water. But best of all, the economy of these islands depends mostly on fish, which make up about sixty percent of all exported goods. So much for eating light—we're feasting!

Island Loafers

2 servings

1 can dark tuna

1 pound ground chicken

1 cup cooked brown rice

1 egg, beaten

1/4 cup fresh chopped parsley

2 tablespoons fresh minced garlic

3 tablespoons wheat germ

1/2 cup chopped carrots

Preheat oven to 350 degrees.

In a large bowl, mix all ingredients. Form into a loaf pan, and bake for 1 hour or until done. Let cool and serve. Slice Island Loafers and serve over kibble.

4

The Middle East

We're so excited to see the Middle East, with its history, mystery and legends.

Egypt

· ·

We always thought Egypt was just one big dry desert, but we found that the Nile Valley was in fact lush and fertile. Tara made friends with one of the few cats I've ever seen who is *bigger* than Tara. She showed us around the pyramids and the countryside and shared her favorite recipe with us. We also saw the biggest cat in the world—the great Sphinx!

FROM THE KITCHEN OF ROBERTA VIGGIANO:

Farik

(CHICKEN AND MEAT SOUP)

8 servings

1 pound chicken pieces

1/2 pound shin veal

1 pound barley

salt

pepper

4 hard-boiled eggs, sliced

Simmer the chicken, shin of veal (cut into approximately 8 pieces), barley, salt and pepper in a pan full of water for 4 to 6 hours until the chicken meat falls off the bone. Remove the bones. Put meat back into soup and add the sliced eggs.

Saudi Arabia

What a different country this is! As females, we were wrapped from head to toe in special veils and robes that covered everything except our eyes. Between the black clothing and the heat of the desert, I thought we were going to die! But those robes could hide a lot of food under them—so we stocked up on goodies!

Arabian Nuggets

20-30 nuggets

1 large can tuna or
mackerel, packed in oil

1 tablespoon chopped parsley

1 cup crushed corn flakes

2 tablespoons wheat germ

Preheat oven to 350 degrees.

Blend tuna or mackerel with parsley, roll into balls. Combine corn flakes and wheat germ. Roll balls in corn flake and wheat germ mixture. Bake on a lightly greased cookie sheet for 7 to 10 minutes until golden brown. Cool and serve. May be stored in the refrigerator.

Israel

We never realized how many tourists visit this small country, but there's a reason why 1.6 million people come here each year—the people are so friendly, and the land is rich in history and culture. And one thing we're learning on this voyage of voyages is that where there's history, there's always a great recipe!

Chicken Liver Pâté

4 servings

2 tablespoons butter or margarine

1/2 pound chicken livers

2 eggs, hard-boiled

Heat butter or margarine in a frying pan. Sauté chicken livers over medium heat, stirring occasionally, for approximately 10 to 15 minutes until cooked through. Chop liver and eggs in a food processor or blender, a little at a time. Mold into shape and serve with Garlic and Anchovy Snaps (see p. 44).

Chicken Soup with Matzo Balls

The twist here is inside your matzo balls, where you add a little piece of sardine. Only in Israel did we find these. They're a cat's dream come true.

6 servings

4 quarts cold water

4 pounds chicken necks, backs and legs

4 chopped carrots

3 stalks of celery with leaves

1 cup chopped parsley

2 bay leaves

Place all ingredients in an 8- to 10-quart broth pot and bring to a boil. Reduce heat and simmer for 2 1/2 hours partially covered. When cool, strain through a colander with some cheese cloth to catch all the bones and vegetables. Place broth in a container, let cool and refrigerate overnight. The next day, the fat will have hardened on top—simply remove. Save 1/2 cup fat for the matzo balls. Soup can be frozen.

Matzo Balls

With a twist . . . try a little fish inside.

6–8 servings

6 eggs

1 tablespoon finely chopped parsley

1/2 cup chicken fat from the top of the soup

1 can sardines

2/3 cup hot water

1 1/2 cups matzo meal

Beat eggs lightly. Slowly add parsley, chicken fat, sardines and water. Slowly add matzo meal. Mix well and refrigerate for 2 hours. Drop the mixture by the spoonful into rapidly boiling soup. Reduce heat and cook for 1 hour, uncovered. Serve at room temperature.

5

Europe

If Mom and Dad could only see us now! Our travel dreams (well, mine at least) are all coming true. So many interesting, different and glamorous countries are in this part of the world.

Greece

Eating in Greece is one of the wildest experiences we've had yet. There we were, peacefully finishing our dinner, when all of a sudden everyone got up and began dancing like crazy! That was fine, but when they started breaking the dishes in some ceremonial frenzy, we ran for our lives. Fortunately, we escaped with a few tasty recipes . . . .

Garlic and Anchovy Snaps

Makes 6–8 dozen

1 pound cooked boneless chicken, white and dark meat

1 can anchovies

2 cloves fresh peeled garlic

1 cup low-salt chicken broth

1 1/2 cups wheat germ

2 tablespoons brewer's yeast (optional)

2 cups whole-wheat flour (more may be needed)

1 cup yellow cornmeal

Garlic powder

Glaze:

Beat 1 egg. Lightly brush on snap before baking.

Preheat oven to 350 degrees.

In a large blender or food processor, gradually purée chicken, anchovies and garlic, while adding chicken broth. Transfer the chicken purée into a large bowl. Mix in wheat germ and brewer's yeast. Slowly add flour and cornmeal until the dough becomes stiff. Knead the dough for 3 to 5 minutes. Let it rest for 5 to 10 minutes. On a lightly floured surface, roll the dough into a ball.

As cats like their snaps thin, I have found that the best way to do this is to split the ball into four sections and roll each section into a hot dog shape. Wrap these in plastic wrap and chill for 30 minutes. Slice into very thin chips. Place the chips on a lightly greased cookie sheet, and brush with glaze. Lightly sprinkle with garlic powder and bake for 25 to 40 minutes. Halfway through, turn. As the snaps cool, they will become hard. Leftover dough can be frozen for up to 3 months.

Greek Shrimp

6 servings

1 tablespoon olive oil

2 teaspoons chopped garlic

1 pound fresh shrimp, peeled and cleaned

1/4 cup chopped parsley

Heat olive oil, sauté garlic until translucent, about 10 minutes. Add shrimp and cook until shrimp are pink. When cool, chop with fresh parsley and serve alone or with some kibble and rice.

Italy

Between the food and the boys, the only thing I can say is . . .
Bellissimo!

Pasta, Pasta, Pasta

6 servings

1/2 pound cooked thin spaghetti

1 can dark tuna with oil

1/4 cup parmesan cheese

1/2 cup bread crumbs

Preheat oven to 350 degrees.

Mix spaghetti, tuna and parmesan cheese. Put into a casserole dish. Sprinkle bread crumbs on top. Bake for 25 to 30 minutes. Cool and serve.

Spain

Olé! We had never seen a bullfight before, so we sneaked into a bull ring thinking we would have a nice evening on the town. Tara fainted so many times I thought we would need a vet, so I got her out of there quickly and revived her spirits with some delicious Spanish cuisine.

Shrimp Empañadas Without Crust

4 servings

1 cup fish broth

1 clove garlic, chopped

3 tablespoons kelp powder

1/4 cup chopped fresh parsley

1/2 pound fresh shrimp, peeled and cleaned

Combine fish broth, garlic, kelp powder and parsley. Place shrimp in frying pan. Pour sauce over shrimp. Simmer for 5 to 10 minutes over medium heat until shrimp is pink and cooked through. Cool, chop and serve over kibble.

Serve at room temperature.

Cookitos

Makes 4–5 dozen

2 cups whole-wheat flour

2/3 cup yellow cornmeal

1/2 cup shelled sunflower seeds

2 tablespoons corn oil

1/2 cup fish broth

2 eggs mixed with 1/4 cup lowfat milk

Glaze:

Beat 1 egg. Lightly brush on cookie before baking.

Preheat oven to 350 degrees.

In a large bowl, mix dry ingredients and seeds together. Add oil, broth and egg mixture. Your dough should be firm. Let sit 15 to 20 minutes. On a lightly floured surface, roll out dough 1/4 inch thick. Cut into shapes and brush with glaze. Bake for 25 to 30 minutes until golden brown. Take out and cool. Store cookies in an airtight container.

Monte Carlo

Ahhh, Dahhling! My diamonds, the famous casino, the royalty and the champagne bubbly all went together splendidly. I went in search of 007. Tara went for the nouvelle cuisine.

Salmon Pâté

4 servings

1 12-ounce can salmon, drained

1 tablespoon olive oil

4 tablespoons cottage cheese

Blend all ingredients in a blender or food processor. Mold and chill until firm.

Serve at room temperature.

Carrot Bisque

2 1/2 cups fish broth

5 small carrots, chopped

1 clove garlic, chopped

2/3 cup powdered nonfat milk

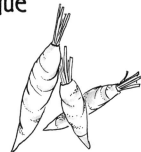

Combine broth, carrots and garlic. Boil and reduce to a simmer. Cook for 15 to 20 minutes. Drain and reserve liquid.

Purée carrots and garlic. Add powdered milk and blend. Slowly add purée to fish broth and blend well. Serve over kitty kibble.

Shrimp Remoulade Sauce

6-8 servings

2 hard-boiled eggs, mashed

1 teaspoon anchovy paste

1/2 cup cottage cheese

2 tablespoons chopped parsley

2 cloves garlic, chopped

1 pound boiled shrimp

Blend first five ingredients. Serve over chopped warm shrimp.

England

More royalty! And more food! Today I had to let my collar out another notch because it was getting so tight. Tara complained about the damp, cold weather. We both agreed, however, that the Brits have a wonderful tradition of "tea time" with quite the selection of cakes and goodies. Best of all, we liked being called "M'Lady!" wherever we went.

Tea Time Snack

The best cookies we ever had!

Makes 3–4 dozen

3 cups whole-wheat flour

1 cup yellow cornmeal

1 cup rolled oats

2/3 cup nonfat dry milk

1 can chopped clams

2 tablespoons garlic powder

1 1/2 cups clam juice

1/2 cup corn oil

2 eggs

Glaze:

Beat 1 egg. Lightly brush on cookie before baking.

Preheat oven to 350 degrees.

Mix flour, cornmeal, oats, dry milk, clams and garlic powder in a large bowl. Form a well in the middle of the mixture. Whisk clam juice, corn oil and two eggs in another bowl. Stir this into flour mixture and blend until a stiff dough forms. An extra 1/4 to 1/2 cup of whole-wheat flour can be added if the dough is not stiff enough. Let dough rest for 20 to 25 minutes. Roll out dough on a floured surface as thin as possible. Cut dough into shapes with your favorite cookie cutters. Brush with glaze. Bake for 25 to 30 minutes. Store cookies in an airtight container.

Liver and Bacon

4 servings

1 pound lamb liver

flour

1/2 pound bacon

1 beef bouillon cube, diluted in 1 cup water

Dip liver in flour. Coat on both sides. Cook bacon and remove to plate. Drain fat. Cook liver in same pan, 5 minutes on each side. Remove liver. Combine 1/2 cup flour with beef bouillon and add to the pan and de-glaze. Stir until gravy thickens. Add gravy over liver. Crumble bacon over the top. Cool to room temperature and serve.

Braised Ox Tongue

10-20 servings

1 ox tongue

1 clove garlic

salt

1 carrot, peeled

Blanch the ox tongue in boiling water, then rinse in cold water. Crush the garlic clove with salt and cut the carrot in small pieces. Put both in a saucepan. Add the tongue, cover with cold water and bring to a boil. Simmer covered for 2 to 3 hours. Remove the tongue from the pan, skin it and keep hot while boiling up and reducing the liquid. Put tongue back in the saucepan. Cook until tender. Serve with the sauce poured over it.

Liver Drops

6 servings

5 cups water

1 chicken bouillon cube

1 pound chicken livers

1 cup seasoned bread crumbs mixed with 2 tablespoons wheat germ

Combine water and bouillon cube into a large saucepan and bring to a boil. Add liver and boil until tender. Drain. Take liver and place in blender or food processor. Blend until mixture is stiff with small chunks; form into small balls. Roll meatballs in bread-crumb mixture. Place on a lightly greased cookie sheet and bake until golden brown. Let liver drops cool and serve. This may be frozen in single-serving portions.

Norway

It's much colder here, but Tara and I have built up quite a
layer of insulation—and the people are very warm and friendly.
Norway is famous for its salmon, and we are sampling it in
every way possible. The salmon loaf is the best so far.

Salmon Loaf

6 servings

1 16-ounce can of salmon, with liquid from can

1/2 cup milk

3 cups bread crumbs

1/4 cup butter

3 egg yolks, beaten

2 tablespoons julienne carrots

1 teaspoon crushed garlic

3 egg whites, stiffly beaten

Preheat oven to 350 degrees

Drain and flake salmon, save liquid.

Heat milk, add bread crumbs and butter. Let stand for a few minutes. Add salmon liquid and beat. Add egg yolks, carrots, garlic and salmon. Mix well.

Fold in egg whites and pour into well-greased baking dish or loaf pan. Bake for 45 to 50 minutes. Let rest when out of oven before turning on to platter. Then cool, slice and serve.

Liver and Garlic Crisps

Makes 6–8 dozen

1 pound cooked chicken livers, boiled

1 clove garlic, chopped

1 cup low-salt beef broth

1 1/2 cups wheat germ

2 tablespoons brewer's yeast (optional)

1 cup yellow cornmeal

2 cups whole-wheat flour

Glaze:

Beat 1 egg. Lightly brush on crisps before baking.

Preheat oven to 350 degrees.

Using a blender or food processor, purée the liver and garlic while slowly adding beef broth. When all the liver is puréed, transfer to a large bowl. Blend in wheat germ and brewer's yeast. Slowly add cornmeal and whole-wheat flour until the dough becomes stiff. Knead dough for 3 to 5 minutes and let it rest for an additional 5 minutes. On a lightly floured surface, roll the dough into a ball.

For thin crackers: Roll the ball into four sections and roll each section into a hot dog shape. Wrap these in plastic wrap and chill for 30 minutes. Slice into very thin chips. Place the chips on a lightly greased cookie sheet (I always use cooking spray when lightly greasing my cookie sheets), and brush with glaze. Bake for 25 to 40 minutes. Halfway through, turn. As the crackers cool, they will become hard. Leftover dough can be frozen for up to 3 months.

Norwegian "Gold" Fish

1 12-ounce can of salmon

1 egg

1 tablespoon fresh chopped parsley

1 tablespoon kelp powder

1 tablespoon wheat germ

1 2/3 cups unbleached flour

1 clove garlic, chopped

Preheat oven to 350 degrees.

Drain salmon (save liquid). Blend all ingredients, add the salmon juice a little at a time if the dough is dry. Let rest for 5 minutes. Flour the board and roll out to 1/4 to 1/2 inches thick. Cut into shapes (fish shapes are fun if you have a fish-shaped cookie cutter). Bake for 25 to 30 minutes. Cool and serve. Can be stored in refrigerator or freezer.

6

The Caribbean

Tara and I had heard something about pirates in the Caribbean, but ashore we met many friendly islanders who showed us around and never once made us walk a plank. And with all of the calypso dancing we've been doing, we've actually gotten a little exercise!

Jamaica

Jamaica was wet and wild. We kept getting lost in all the lush vegetation. The "cats" were just too "kool" and we had a blast. Music, music everywhere—they call it reggae. What a party! We danced all night and loved the food.

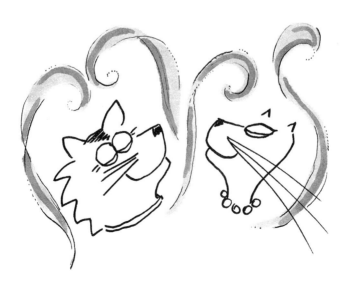

Jerk Chicken

We loved this dish. We just ordered it without the spice.

2 servings

1 clove garlic, crushed

1/4 teaspoon dark brown sugar

1/4 teaspoon orange juice

1/4 teaspoon soy sauce

1/4 cup olive oil

1 boneless chicken breast, cut into strips

Blend garlic, sugar, orange juice, soy sauce and olive oil. Add chicken to marinate for 30 minutes. Grill over an open barbecue until done (about 25 minutes).

Serve over a bed of warm brown rice.

All over the island we could smell food grilling. Our noses were working overtime!

Island Grilled Red Snapper

2 servings

1 small whole red snapper, cleaned

olive oil

1 small lime, halved

1/4 cup chopped parsley

Clean fish, brush with olive oil. Place on a hot grill inside or outside. Squeeze lime juice and sprinkle parsley over fish while cooking. Cook 4 minutes per side. Cool and serve.

St. Thomas

I wanted to try snorkeling, but Tara would have nothing of it. She was up for trying some of the different regional dishes, which we both purred over.

Caribbean Fish Stew

6 servings

1/2 pound bacon

1/4 pound okra, chopped

2 cloves garlic, chopped

1 can anchovies, packed in oil

2 cans chopped clams

1/4 pound fresh shrimp, cut into pieces

1/4 pound fresh red snapper, cut into pieces

1/4 pound fresh sea scallops, cut into cubes

3 cups fish stock

In a large stock pot cook bacon until light brown. Remove bacon and set aside. Add okra and garlic to pot. Cook for 10 minutes over low heat. Add anchovies with oil, clams with juice, shrimp, red snapper and sea scallops. Add the fish stock. Bring to a boil and then simmer for 30 minutes, partially uncovered. Cool and serve. This dish is *so* good on it's own.

St. Thomas Nibblers

2-4 dozen nibblers

1 can sardines, packed in oil

1/2 cup parmesan cheese

1 cup cornmeal

1 egg, beaten

Preheat oven to 325 degrees.

Blend sardines, parmesan cheese and cornmeal. Add egg and mix well. Drop by 1/2 teaspoon onto greased cookie sheet. Bake 7 to 10 minutes. Cool and serve. May be frozen for later use. Will keep for several days in airtight container in refrigerator.

Cuba

Cuba is the largest island of the West Indies, and it's known for its agricultural products. Of course, where there is

agriculture, there is food! Unfortunately for me, I tried smoking a famous Cuban cigar. Aside from burning one of my whiskers, it made me feel absolutely terrible.

Cuban Steak

6 servings

1/4 cup orange juice

3 cloves garlic, crushed

1/4 teaspoon lime juice

1 small flank steak

Blend orange juice, garlic and lime juice in a blender. Pour over steak to marinate for 1 hour. Grill or broil until medium rare. Slice into small pieces and serve warm over some kibble.

7

The U.S.A.

Key West

Back in the U.S.A.! Back on home turf, it is sure nice to find some good old all-American meals! We miss Mom and Dad, and can't wait to somehow find our way home!

We had to be careful ashore here for fear that an alligator might spot us. At this point, we would make for one heck of a meal ourselves, and we're in no shape to outrun them.

Tuna Loaf

6 servings

1 large can tuna

1/2 cup milk

3 cups bread crumbs

1/4 cup butter

1/3 cup tuna liquid saved from can

3 egg yolks, beaten

1 teaspoon crushed garlic

3 egg whites, stiffly beaten

Preheat oven to 350 degrees.

Drain and flake tuna, save liquid. Heat milk, add bread crumbs and butter. Let stand for a few minutes. Add tuna liquid and beat. Add egg yolks, garlic and tuna. Mix well.

Fold in egg whites and pour into well-greased baking dish or loaf pan. Bake at 350 degrees for 45 to 50 minutes. Let rest when out of oven before turning on to platter. Then cool, slice and serve.

Shrimp Crunchies

Makes 3–4 dozen

3 cups whole-wheat flour

1 cup yellow cornmeal

1 cup rolled oats

2/3 cup nonfat dry milk

1/2 cup dried shrimp, ground

2 tablespoons garlic powder

1 1/2 cups clam juice

1/2 cup corn oil

2 eggs

Glaze:

Beat 1 egg. Lightly brush on crunchies before baking.

Preheat oven to 350 degrees.

Mix flour, cornmeal, oats, dry milk, dried shrimp and garlic powder in a large bowl. Form a well in the middle of the mixture. Whisk clam juice, corn oil and two eggs in another bowl. Stir this into flour mixture and blend until a stiff dough forms. An extra 1/4 to 1/2 cup of whole-wheat flour can be added if the dough is not stiff enough. Let the dough rest for 20 to 25 minutes. Roll out dough on a floured surface; try to keep it as thin as possible. Cut dough into shapes with your favorite cookie cutter. Brush with glaze. Bake for 25 to 30 minutes. Store cookies in an airtight container.

Kitty Cubes

This recipe is quick, easy and fun. We had never had any-thing like them, and they were wonderful for cooling us off and quenching our thirst from the hot Florida sun. These might best be served outside to avoid water on your carpet.

Makes 24–36 cubes

2/3 cup water

2 cups beef, chicken or fish broth

2–3 ice-cube trays

Mix water with beef, chicken or fish broth. Pour into ice trays. Place in freezer and serve cubes as needed.

NOTE: Even though cats don't tend to like food served cold, they do generally like to play with and chew on ice cubes. Once the cubes start to melt, they get interested. Natural food colorings can be added. Ice cubes are especially helpful dur-ing summer months, as they keep the drinking water cool and the cat hydrated.

For Teething Kittens: Rubbing ice cubes on your kitten's gums can help relieve those pains associated with new teeth and often diminish teething tendencies. Wrapping the ice cubes in a clean rag also provides your little one with a fun toy.

New Orleans

The last stop on our cruise! New Orleans is a Louisiana city on the Gulf of Mexico. Founded in 1718, this city has a very French flavor, and the cats here sure know how to party. Their most famous party, of course, is Mardi Gras, which is two weeks of non-stop celebrating! This town is also the birthplace of jazz, so the music never stops. When we got off the boat, the sights, sounds and smells were buzzing. The air was filled with the smell of fish cooking and beignets frying. What a marvelous mix of French and American cultures. We didn't sleep a wink!

Catfish Drops

Makes 20-30 drops

1/2 pound dried catfish (or cod if you can't find catfish)

1/2 cup parmesan cheese

1/2 cup cornmeal

1 egg, beaten

Preheat oven to 325 degrees.

Put the catfish or cod in a bowl, add boiling water and let sit for 20 to 30 minutes. Drain and then mix with parmesan cheese, cornmeal and beaten egg.

Drop by 1 teaspoon on a greased cookie sheet. Bake for 7 to 10 minutes. Cool and serve. May be stored in an airtight container in refrigerator or freezer.

8

The Great
Train Ride

Home to Long Beach

Left in New Orleans with no way home, Tara was in a state of sheer panic and, I must admit, even I was a bit nervous. Then she did something that really surprised me. For the first time in her life, she took off on her own to find us a way home while I, for once, waited. When she returned hours later with news of a train leaving that night for Long Beach and a plan to sneak us on board, I almost died! This trip had really changed Tara for the better.

Fortunately, her plan to hop the train worked. Once aboard we befriended a woman who snuck us food during the trip—ham-and-cheese sandwiches wrapped in plastic. Not much, considering the fine cuisine we'd been dining on, but in the mornings she treated us to "choo choo chewies" which we promptly devoured.

Train Cuisine

Choo Choo Chewies

Makes 20–30 chewies

1 can sardines

1/4 cup brown rice

1/4 cup chopped parsley

1/4 cup grated cheese

1 cup bread crumbs mixed with 2 tablespoons wheat germ

Preheat oven to 350 degrees.

Blend sardines, brown rice, parsley and cheese together. Roll into balls and then dip and roll in bread-crumb mixture. Bake on lightly greased cookie sheet for 7 to 10 minutes until light brown. Cool and serve. May be stored in an airtight container in the freezer or refrigerator.

The End of a Journey

When we finally found our way home from the train station, Mom and Dad were shocked and overjoyed to see us. They had given us up for lost, but upon seeing our overstuffed bodies and healthy coats, they knew we had been safe and well-cared for.

We've spent many hours telling our "tail" around the neighborhood, but I'm not sure anyone believes us.

So much has changed. I've come to love home life much more now—I really appreciate sitting in the window sill savoring the memories of my travels. Tara has become a little bolder and even ventures outside on her own every now and then. Along our journey we came to understand each other better and appreciate our differences. What a special friend my Tara is, and what an amazing adventure we had together!

Now it's home sweet home . . . and with all our new recipes, we'll *never* leave home again!

chapter 9

The Saucy Cat

This section offers you some great suggestions on how to vary the flavor of your cat's everyday mainstay kibble. Instead of buying a new brand of cat food or kibble, try adding a gravy to spruce things up and stimulate appetite.

When adding a gravy or sauce to kibble, mix well so your cat doesn't just eat the sauce. Adding small amounts to your cat's regular kibble gives great extra flavor without altering his diet.

Chicken or Beef Broth Gravy

2 cups chicken or beef broth

2 tablespoons cornstarch

In a sauce pan, add the cornstarch to the broth and bring to a boil. Thicken. Serve at room temperature.

Turkey Gravy

2 tablespoons all-purpose flour

2 tablespoons drippings from a roasted turkey

2 cups boiling water

1/2 cup cooked chopped giblets (optional)

Over medium heat, blend flour and drippings to create a roux (thick paste). Slowly add boiling water while whisking until gravy thickens. Add giblets.

Conversion
Tables

Liquid Measures

American Cup	Imperial Cup
1/4 cup	4 tablespoons
1/3 cup	5 tablespoons
1/2 cup	8 tablespoons
2/3 cup	1/4 pint
3/4 cup	1/4 pint and 2 tablespoons
1 cup	1/4 pint and 6 tablespoons
1 1/4 cups	1/2 pint
1 1/2 cups	1/2 pint and 4 tablespoons
2 cups	3/4 pint
2 1/2 cups	1 pint
3 cups	1 1/2 pints
4 cups	1 1/2 pints and 4 tablespoons
5 cups	2 pints

Solid Measures

American	Imperial
Butter	
1 tablespoon	1/2 ounce
1/4 cup	2 ounces
1/2 cup	4 ounces
1 cup	8 ounces
Cheese (grated)	
1/2 cup	2 ounces
Corn meal	
1 cup	6 ounces
Flour	
1/4 cup	1 1/4 ounces
1/2 cup	2 1/2 ounces
1 cup	5 ounces
1 1/2 cups	7 1/2 ounces
2 cups	10 ounces

American	Imperial
Herbs	
1/4 cup	1/4 ounce
Sugar	
1/4 cup	1 3/4 ounces
1/2 cup	3 ounces
1 cup	6 1/2 ounces
Vegetables	
1/2 cup	2 ounces
1 cup	4 ounces
Wheat Germ	
1/2 cup	1 1/2 ounces
1 cup	3 ounces

Oven Temperatures

	°F	Gas Mark	°C
Cool	225–250	1/4–1/2	110–120
Very Slow	250–275	1/2–1	120–140
Slow	275–300	1–2	140–150
Very Moderate	300–350	2–3	150–160
Moderate	375	4	180
Moderately Hot	400	5–6	190–200
Hot	425–450	7–8	220–230
Very Hot	450–475	8–9	230–240

Ingredient Names

All-purpose flour = Plain flour

Brown sugar = Soft brown sugar

Baking soda = Bicarbonate of soda

Molasses = Treacle

INDEX

Add Your Own Recipes

Send Us Your Recipes

Please send us your suggestions for healthy recipes.

If there is a lipsmacking response, we will include these—with your permission—in our next book.